Archaeopteryx

Written by Rupert Oliver
Illustrated by Bernard Long

Library of Congress Cataloging in Publication Data

Oliver, Rupert.
  Archaeopteryx

  Summary: Describes the physical characteristics,
habits, and natural environment of the winged dinosaur
known as Archaeopteryx.
  1. Archaeopteryx—Juvenile literature. [1. Archaeopteryx. 2. Dinosaurs] I. Long, Bernard, ill.
II. Title.
QE872.A8O45 1984   567.9'7   84-17792
ISBN 0-86592-209-8

Rourke Enterprises, Inc.
Vero Beach, FL 32964

Rhamphorhynchus

Pteranodon

Pterodactyl

Ankylosaurus

Dimetrodon

Iguanodon

Tricondon

Archaeopteryx

Archaeopteryx

Ichthyosaurus

Plesiosaurus

Deinonychus

Nothosaurus

Archaeopteryx woke from her sleep and stretched her wings. She had been asleep since the previous evening and felt rested and full of energy. She moved from the nook in which she had been sleeping and climbed up the tree trunk. Using her clawed hands and feet, Archaeopteryx was able to scramble up the smooth tree trunk.

Archaeopteryx was hungry so she began looking for something to eat. She could not see anything so she climbed higher up the tree. From her new position Archaeopteryx looked down on the branches below. On the upper side of one of these branches was a lizard, perhaps that would make a tasty meal.

Carefully, Archaeopteryx shifted her position, trying not to disturb the lizard. To land close to the lizard, Archaeopteryx would have to launch herself properly. Once she was airborne, Archaeopteryx could not change direction very easily. She was a very awkward flyer. She would have to time the glide down perfectly.

At last Archaeopteryx was satisfied with her position. She spread her feathered wings wide and leapt into the air. Suddenly the lizard saw Archaeopteryx above it. In fear the lizard began to run away, but it was too late. Archaeopteryx landed just inches from the lizard. In a flash she had snapped the lizard up with her sharp teeth.

Archaeopteryx held the lizard beneath her feet. She bit chunks off the reptile and swallowed them whole. Archaeopteryx could hear heavy footsteps on the ground far below, but she did not take any notice. She was about halfway through her meal when a loud rustling among the leaves startled her. Something large was moving among the branches. Anxiously, Archaeopteryx looked round but the noise had stopped. Perhaps it had only been the wind.

Then an enormous shape pushed through the leaves towards Archaeopteryx. It was larger than the whole of Archaeopteryx. Archaeopteryx was suddenly very frightened. She could only think of one thing to do. She leapt from the branch and spread her wings.

Archaeopteryx fluttered down through the air.
As she glided she looked round. The head that had
startled her so much belonged to an enormous
Pelorosaurus. The giant dinosaur was munching
away at the leaves, using its long neck to reach the
upper branches.

Archaeopteryx reached the ground safe and sound. The Pelorosaurus was a planteater and would not bother Archaeopteryx. She scampered into the bushes to avoid the feet of the dinosaur.

Then Archaeopteryx heard other footsteps approaching. They sounded lighter than those of Pelorosaurus, perhaps they belonged to a smaller dinosaur. Suddenly a ferocious Megalosaurus appeared from the undergrowth. The Pelorosaurus saw the mighty hunter and gave a bellow of fear. The huge Pelorosaurus lumbered off through the trees with the powerful Megalosaurus chasing close behind.

When the large dinosaur had gone, Archaeopteryx crept out of the bushes and moved on.

A large, colorful butterfly flew past Archaeopteryx. Archaeopteryx was still hungry and a juicy butterfly would be very tasty. The butterfly flitted on through the bushes. Archaeopteryx stood high on her long legs and scampered after it. Keeping the brightly colored insect in sight, Archaeopteryx pushed through the bushes. Before long she had caught up with the insect. Archaeopteryx leapt high into the air and caught the butterfly in her jaws.

As she crunched the butterfly in her jaws Archaeopteryx turned her head. Not far away the bushes thinned out. Archaeopteryx could smell water. She crept through the bushes looking for a drink.

Archaeopteryx found
herself on a river bank. It was a broad river with wide
banks. The sudden glare of sunlight made
Archaeopteryx blink, but she soon saw that the
riverbanks were crowded with all sorts of animals.

Not far from where she stood a large crocodile
lay half in the water. It was basking in the sunlight
after eating a good meal. Wading in the shallows
were a pair of Elaphrosaurs. Suddenly one of the
Elaphrosaurs plunged its head into the water. When
it came up, Archaeopteryx could see that the
Elaphrosaurus had a fish in its jaw.

A sudden flurry of movement on the bank made Archaeopteryx very nervous. Two male Dryosaurs were fighting. Nearby a female Dryosaurus watched the fight. Archaeopteryx watched as the males kicked each other. Finally, one stopped fighting and moved away. The winner strutted over to the female and moved off with her. It was the breeding season and the fight had decided which was the dominant male. Then something more interesting caught Archaeopteryx's eye.

Not far away was a dead Alocodon. It looked
as if a larger dinosaur had killed the small
planteater. Part of the Alocodon had already been
eaten, but there was enough meat left for
Archaeopteryx.

Cautiously Archaeopteryx approached. Perhaps the hunter that had killed Alocodon was still nearby. Archaeopteryx looked round carefully, but there was nothing in sight. She began to pull at the carcass and was soon enjoying a good meal. Archaeopteryx had just bitten off a juicy piece of meat when a Compsognathus arrived. The small dinosaur wanted the piece of meat that Archaeopteryx had. The two began to squabble over it. Archaeopteryx was trying to hold on to it and Compsognathus was trying to snatch it away.

It was then that Archaeopteryx realized another dinosaur was nearby. Running towards Archaeopteryx and the Compsognathus was a Teinurosaurus. It was the Teinurosaurus that had killed the Alocodon and it was coming to protect its food.

Archaeopteryx knew that if the Teinurosaurus caught her she might end up as another meal, so she ran off as fast as she could. Archaeopteryx's legs could cover ground very quickly, but Teinurosaurus could run even faster. The large dinosaur began to catch up with Archaeopteryx. There was only one chance of escape for Archaeopteryx and she took it. She took a running jump at a huge tree trunk. Archaeopteryx grabbed hold of the bark and quickly scrambled up the tree. She could feel Teinurosaurus just behind her, but the large dinosaur could not climb trees and Archaeopteryx was safe.

The Teinurosaurus glared angrily up at
Archaeopteryx, but it could not reach her so it went
away. It was beginning to get dark now and
Archaeopteryx was tired. She climbed further up the
tree. Soon she found a comfortable fork in the tree
and settled down to sleep for the night. As she rested
a Camptosaurus arrived and began to browse on the
leaves. The sun slowly sank lower in the sky and
Archaeopteryx fell asleep.

Archaeopteryx and Jurassic Europe

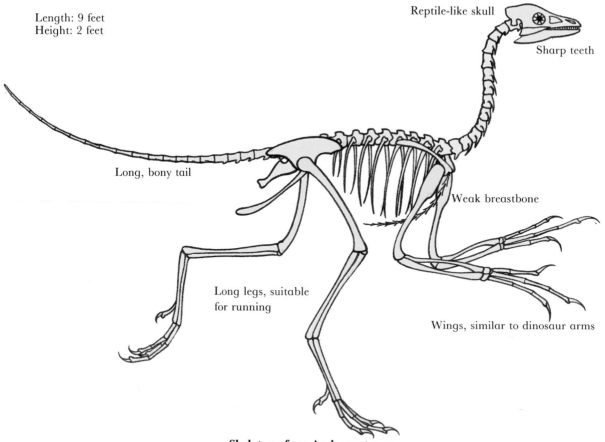

Length: 9 feet
Height: 2 feet

Reptile-like skull

Sharp teeth

Long, bony tail

Weak breastbone

Long legs, suitable for running

Wings, similar to dinosaur arms

Skeleton of an Archaeopteryx

When did Archaeopteryx live?

Archaeopteryx lived during the Age of the Dinosaurs. Scientists have divided this Age into three periods, First the Triassic which began about 225 million years ago and lasted for 35 million years. Next the Jurassic which lasted from 190 million years ago until 136 million years ago. The last period of the Age of Dinosaurs is called the Cretaceous period and lasted until about 64 million years ago. Fossils of Archaeopteryx have been found in rocks that date from about halfway through the Jurassic.

Where did Archaeopteryx live?

All the fossils of Archaeopteryx have been found in a rather small area of Germany. We therefore deduce that it lived in central Europe during the Jurassic. However, the bones of Archaeopteryx are very small and fragile. It is possible that this early bird lived in other parts of the world, but that it was only fossilised in Germany. A mid-Jurassic fossil has been found in North America which may belong to a relative of Archaeopteryx. Unfortunately nobody is sure that it was a bird.

The life of Archaeopteryx

Ever since the first fossil of Archaeopteryx was found in 1861, scientists have been trying to decide how it lived. There have been many suggestions and even today scientists do not all agree with each other. There are two main theories about the life style of this early bird.

The first theory sees Archaeopteryx as a tree-living animal. Archaeopteryx had curved, sharp claws on its front and hind limbs. Such claws would be useful for clinging to tree trunks and branches. Furthermore the big toe grew in such a way that it could be used for holding onto branches. The wing muscles of Archaeopteryx were surprisingly weak. There was no way that it could take off from the ground. The best Archaeopteryx could manage would have been a short glide from a tree branch. The picture that emerges from this evidence is of a tree-climber that could glide to escape danger or catch prey.

However, some scientists point out that the legs of Archaeopteryx are built for fast running on the ground. They also point out that the broad wings could have been used as insect traps or for display purposes. These scientists picture Archaeopteryx as living on the ground, eating insects and scavenging. They also suppose that feathers did not evolve to aid flight. They think that they developed as insulation to keep Archaeopteryx warm and only later were used for flight. In this book we have shown Archaeopteryx in both these roles.

The ancestors of Archaeopteryx

Archaeopteryx was a remarkable animal. It was the earliest bird that we know of, yet in many ways it was more like a reptile than a bird. It had teeth, a bony tail and a rather small breastbone, with no deep keel of bone for the attachment of flying muscles. It has often been said that Archaeopteryx is really a reptile that is halfway through evolving into a bird. The fossils of Archaeopteryx prove that birds evolved from reptiles millions of years ago. Unfortunately scientists cannot agree as to which type of reptile evolved into birds.

Some scientists point out that the creatures that became crocodiles could have become birds, others think that we have not yet found any fossils of the reptiles that became birds. A recent theory states that birds evolved from a type of dinosaur. There was a group of small, running dinosaurs called coelurosaurs whose skeletons were very like that of Archaeopteryx. Compsognathus and Teinurosaurus were both coelurosaurs. The new theory states that Archaeopteryx evolved from dinosaurs like Compsognathus. Nobody has yet been able to prove any of these theories and the ancestors of Archaeopteryx remain unknown.

The world of Archaeopteryx

Europe in mid-Jurassic times was very different from modern Europe. The forests were made up of cycads, conifers, giant ferns and strange plants called Williamsonias. There were no true flowering plants. The animals were just as unfamiliar. The only mammals to be seen were tiny shrew-like creatures which probably only ventured forth at night.

Several species of Pelorosaurus are known to have existed, but from the fragmentary remains found so far, an accurate size of this dinosaur is not known. It was probably about 50 feet long. It lived on vegetation and was hunted by such fearsome dinosaurs as Megalosaurus. This 20 foot long meat-eater was a powerful killer. Dryosaurus was about 10 feet long. It was one of the earliest of the Ornithopods, a group of dinosaurs that later became important. There were several species of Elaphrosaurus, one up to 20 feet long. Elaphrosaurus was an ostrich dinosaur, related to the coelurosaurs. Some of the animals of the Jurassic would be familiar, among them the lizard and butterfly caught by Archaeopteryx. While Archaeopteryx was a poor flier, there was one group of animals that had conquered the air, the pterosaurs. Rhamphorhynchus, a type of pterosaur, can be seen on page 15.

Some present-day descendants of Archaeopteryx

Owl

Eagle

Sparrow

Bird of Paradise